I'm a Great Big
MONSTER TRUCK!

by Michael Anthony Steele
Illustrated by Isidre and Marc Mones

SCHOLASTIC INC.

New York   Toronto   London   Auckland   Sydney

Mexico City   New Delhi   Hong Kong   Buenos Aires

HASBRO and its logo and TONKA are trademarks of Hasbro and are used with permission. © 2004 Hasbro. All Rights Reserved.

Published by Scholastic Inc.
SCHOLASTIC and associated logos are trademarks and/or registered trademarks of Scholastic Inc.

ISBN 0-439-54836-5

10   06 07 08 9/0

Designed by Carisa Swenson

Printed in the U.S.A.
First printing, April 2004

I wait in a special area before the show.

They clean my body and check my great big tires.

I can hear the crowd already. I'm so excited!

Some monster trucks do special tricks.

This truck can turn into a giant robot!

Watch him crush old cars with his great big claws!

As for me, I'm the best at racing other monster trucks!

I'm in the lead when we jump over a row of old cars!

In a freestyle event, I crush old cars any way I want!